ROCKY MOUNTAIN NATIONAL PARK
A Wilderness for All

Photographers Bill Bonebrake, Dick Dietrich, Gene Putney, Glenn Randall, Keith Ladzinski, Kaz Hagiwara, Laurence Parent, Les Moore, Mary Liz Austin, Ron Maurer, Scott T. Smith, Tom & Pat Leeson, Willard Clay and Willy Onarheim

Text by Judy Rosen

ISBN: 978-1-56540-090-0

Second Printing, December 2009

4961 Windplay Drive, El Dorado Hills, CA 95762
www.impactphotographics.com

Printed in China

Mountains are like magnets, drawing people to their heights. But of all our nation's mountains, what makes these so special? Perhaps nowhere are they more accessible than in Rocky Mountain National Park. In fact, you can reach the mountaintops – and a treeless world of alpine tundra reminiscent of the Arctic – in less than an hour's drive up Trail Ridge Road, America's highest continuous paved highway.

Rocky Mountain National Park spans nearly 7,000 feet in elevation, from 7,640 feet to 14,259 feet above sea level.For every thousand feet you climb, the temperature drops three to five degrees Fahrenheit. And each thousand-foot gain in altitude is equivalent to traveling 600 miles north. As you climb upward you encounter three distinct ecosystems – montane, subalpine, and alpine tundra – similar to those found along the way to Canada and Alaska. Indeed, many of the plants in Rocky Mountain National Park also occur above the Arctic Circle.

Rocky Mountain National Park is a wilderness for all travelers, whether sightseeing from your car or scaling the lofty summits. Only an hour and a half drive from Denver and other Front Range cities, the park preserves 416 square miles of spectacular mountain scenery. Over one hundred peaks soar above 10,000 feet. Deer, elk, and moose grace mountain meadows. Coyotes dash through the valleys while bighorn sheep cling to craggy cliffs high above. Lightning cracks the sky during afternoon thunderstorms. It is a place where nature prevails and its drama plays out on a grand scale. In a world of rapidly dwindling wild places, Rocky Mountain National Park is a refuge, not only for the animals that make their homes here, but for all people and all time.

The Never Summer Mountains rise to meet the heavens where alpine sunflowers *(rydbergia)* dot the meadows above treeline.

From 7,640 feet to 14,259 feet above sea level, Rocky Mountain National Park encompasses a remarkable array of plant and animal communities in a short distance. Ecosystems progress from warm montane meadows through cool subalpine forests before giving way to a treeless world of alpine tundra.

Decreasing daylight in autumn triggers aspen leaves to change color and fall, draping the hillsides in rich golden hues.

Dawn casts an early-morning alpenglow on the high peaks where glaciers descended 12,000 years ago, sculpting the stunning valley of Moraine Park.

Montane Ecosystem – Up to 9,500 feet

Your journey into Rocky Mountain National Park begins in sun-dappled meadows fringed by ponderosa pines. Here, the inviting openness of the montane ecosystem hosts a rich variety of shrubs, grasses, and flowers, key to the survival of many species.

A coyote darts through tall grass in pursuit of a meadow vole. A mule deer nibbles on bitterbrush and a golden-mantled ground squirrel scurries into its burrow with cheek-loads of food. A raucous call and flash of bright blue wings announces a Steller's jay.

The montane life zone, dominated by ponderosa pine on south facing slopes, Douglas-fir on north-facing slopes, and interspersed with aspen, is the most diverse ecosystem in the park. From dawn to dusk, you can catch glimpses and hear the chatter of birds and mammals busily making a living.

Perched in a ponderosa pine, the great horned owl watches over the forest, but with its camouflage, is seldom seen.

Aptly named for their large mule-like ears, mule deer are ever alert to impending danger.

Shedding antlers in spring, male elk quickly sprout new ones, encased in a soft, capillary-rich velvet that nourishes and protects the new growth.

The chilling bugle call of a male elk in rut, beginning deep in the throat and rising to a high-pitched squeal, resounds through the valley sending a multi-layered message that attracts females and intimidates other males.

(Left) A tree swallow peeks out from its feather-lined nest inside an aspen trunk.

(Above) Montane meadows are filled with golden-mantled ground squirrels gathering nature's bounty.

(Opposite) Easily identified by their large ears and black-tipped tails, mule deer number about 500 in Rocky Mountain National Park. Only the males have antlers.

Subalpine Ecosystem – 9,500-11,500 feet

Climbing higher, and you ascend into cool, dense forests of narrow-crowned spruce and fir trees rising to the sky. Snow lingers longer in the forest shade and provides a rich understory of wildflowers and cover for secretive animals. Here, the coats of weasels and snowshoe hares turn from winter-white to summer-brown to match their environment, improving their chances in the age-old game of predator and prey.

An enchanted world awaits travelers beneath the forest canopy. As you walk, footsteps are hushed by the damp air and moist, soft ground. Tune in to an orchestra of birds, including the flute-like song of the hermit thrush and the percussion of a three-toed woodpecker. Mountain chickadees chatter and scold from tree limbs above. Wildlife is more often heard than seen in these forests, dark and deep.

(Opposite) Resembling a brush dipped in bright red paint, the Indian paintbrush splashes the forest floor with vivid color.

Rocky Mountain National Park boasts the greatest concentration of wildlife in the southern Rocky Mountains. Elk are frequently seen along Trail Ridge Road.

An accessible 0.6 mile trail wraps around the wooded shoreline of Bear Lake. In the distance, the lyrical Keyboard of the Winds ascends to the blocky summit of 14,259-foot Longs Peak, the highest mountain in the park.

Distinctive Hallett Peak (center) on the crest of the Continental Divide towers over the forests at an elevation of 12,173 feet above sea level.

Krummholz Ecotone – 11,000 to 11,500 feet

Whipped by wind and ice, the spruce and fir trees below now struggle for survival. The transition zone, or ecotone, between tree and treeless is called krummholz, a German word meaning crooked wood.

Higher on Trail Ridge Road, travelers witness the effects of relentless winds and frigid temperatures on tree growth. Trunks twist into unusual shapes. Branches survive on the leeward side of trunks, resembling flags. Trees are dwarfed into shrubs, which, at tree line, give way to a vast expanse of alpine tundra.

24

Alpine Tundra– 11,500 feet and above

Climbing higher still, you reach a land beyond where trees can grow. Mean annual temperatures hover around freezing. Winds blast up to 100 miles per hour. It can snow at any time of the year.

Rocky Mountain National Park protects the largest expanse of accessible alpine tundra in the contiguous United States. With eleven miles of Trail Ridge Road winding above the trees, you can step out of your car and into the rarified air of an arctic-like landscape.

In this land of extremes, alpine dwellers require special adaptations to survive. Plants hug the ground where the air is warmer. They grow hair on stems and leaves as a protective layer for warmth. Many are filled with anthocyanin, a red pigment that converts the intense ultraviolet sun rays to heat. Only with these strategies can they grow and bloom in the few brief months of summer.

Several animals make their homes here year-round. Large furry rodents called marmots are often seen sunning on rocks. The tiny pika thrives in rock piles, an excellent refuge from predators and alpine winds. Bighorn sheep, with horns that grow throughout life, have two-layered coats of wool and down to insulate them on mountain slopes, high above the sights and sounds of people.

The majestic bighorn sheep, the official state mammal of Colorado, is the symbol of Rocky Mountain National Park and the wilderness it protects.

Elk escape the summer's heat in the cool alpine meadows above treeline.

Bright pink petals of moss campion bloom amidst cushions of tiny leaves. Their low compact growth, a common alpine adaptation, shields the plant from fierce winds.

Bighorn sheep are remarkably adapted to the high country, with rubber-like inner hooves that enable them to cling to steep cliffs and keen vision equal to high-powered binoculars.

Snow-dusted peaks thrust high above the clouds over Forest Canyon.

Longs Peak, the highest summit in the park, rises 14,259 feet above sea level.

During the short alpine summer marmots play, sun on rocks, and eat enough to double their weight. The fat they put on during this crucial period sustains them through winter hibernation.

A diminutive relative of the rabbit, the pika thrives in rock piles of the alpine tundra – an environment that provides a well-camouflaged hiding place for these busy creatures.

The industrious pika stockpiles up to 50 pounds of grass each summer to sustain itself though the winter. Its short round ears reduce the loss of vital heat in the frigid alpine air.

The elusive forest-dwelling black bear is a rare sight in open meadows above treeline.

Lakes shimmer like jewels set into forests, mountainsides, and rocky basins in the lush subalpine forest below the treeless tundra.

Plunging from the heights, cascades race down the mountainside, nourishing the valleys below.

The Colorado River, with its headwaters atop the Continental Divide, meanders lazily through the Kawuneeche Valley on the park's west side.

The wide open wetlands of the Kawuneeche Valley are ideal habitat for the sandhill crane. This nine-mile long valley supports only one breeding pair.

Moose are most frequently spotted in the park's Kawuneechee Valley. Just hours old, a newborn moose calf rises with the help of its mother.

Male moose stand seven feet high at the shoulder and can weigh up to 1200 pounds. Bulbous snouts, flattened antlers, and dark brown fur distinguish them as they graze among the willows beside meandering streams.

Winter offers a subtle beauty beneath a silent cloak of snow. This is an ideal time to explore the wonders of a sleepier season. Rocky Mountain National Park awaits your discovery; its wilderness is accessible in all seasons… for all travelers, all time.